Coffee Traveller
Texts \ Monologues

Fahad Ben. G

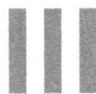

III Clink Street

London | New York

Published by Clink Street Publishing 2019

Copyright © 2019

Cover photo by the Saudi Artist Tagreed AlBagshi
artbagshi@yahoo.com

First edition.

ISBN:
978-1-913136-38-3 - paperback
978-1-913136-39-0 - ebook

To those who forever departed our lives, yet their memories, voices, and whispers remained in our memories forever, too.

Incomplete introduction

No more than attempts:
I am not a writer. I am just a simple person who likes writing. Some people like to express themselves through clothes, cars, dogs, haircut, tattoo, or even the way they laugh! I like to express myself through writing . When I write, I feel things around me more, and more. I feel people around me too. And when I feel them, I feel alive, because I write about these feelings. Sometimes I like writing to others more than talking to them! Because I think in that way I give them more time to understand and get what I mean! Also they can read it twice or even more before they react to it , and maybe their reaction will change after the second reading, or third , or even fourth, who knows!

Sometimes I write to give myself another chance to live with the people on whom I write. I time travel to them and tell them what I could not say back then.

And some other times I write to myself… about stuck things that refuse to leave and refuse to stay! I release them through writing then I set them permanently free on paper.

I write about true feelings that I do not feel ashamed of. They are feelings that do not indicate weakness or strength. They refer to an ability to feel things and comprehend people around me. I translate that feeling then as it is and as I feel it on paper without any modification or editing. I write about things that happened to all of us. We all have lived them without writing about them. I write about a feeling because I know well that feeling people and things around me is a bless bestowed upon me from God. Writing honestly about that feeling is a challenge for me in front of myself.

I write about feelings that can be experienced and cannot be said because they will die if they were spoken. Therefore, I decided to write them down so that they would live on paper and in the minds of each reader.

I write honestly because I know that what I write is going to reach the heart of all those who read it honestly, too.

The kind of writing I compose
Each person has their own way and style that suits them in writing. I write in one style and I discovered later that it is so close to something called in literature *the stream of consciousness*.

The stream of consciousness (definition as I understand it from my readings):
It is a kind mental flow of speech or a spontaneous, internal, pictorial monologue that nobody except the writer hears or feels, so the author transmits it on paper in their own way as scattered texts so that all people will read it.

So, I realized that I am using a flow of ideas and an internal, incoherent dialogue related to different people, places, and times of my life that I have decided to bring into light. I realized too that When we reconcile with our memory, we make friends with it without our knowledge or awareness. The bad part of it shall strengthen us and changes slowly over time to lesson we draw benefit and learn from them However, when we fight it and marginalize its events, it will remain an obsession that haunts us, and we will remain on the run from it throughout our lives. At certain unexpected moments in our lives, it will slay us.

Personally, I think We resort to our memory each time we decide to meet ourselves or other people because when we love, we see our reflection in and on the people whom we love, and that leads us to one fact which is We are a mixture of infinite memories which has a big impact in choosing things and people around us whether we like it or not.

The memory does not betray... the memory does not betray at all.

Fahad
1/5/2017 2:15 am
Opposite to Azumi Garden Building –
Tokyo - Japan

Sometime the heart bleeds more than our tribe permits and further than traditions tolerate. However, it is internal bleeding only.

(A scene)

I was eight years old…

I rushed to the flower shop at the corner of the street.

I emptied my pockets before the shopkeeper.

He sympathized…

I brought you a lovely bouquet

Of red flowers wrapped in paper and love.

I wrote to you on the note with the most terrible handwriting,

"You are the fairest in the universe, and you will become more and more beautiful."

You took the bouquet;

You shed violet tears after you read the note.

Until now, I do not forget the scene –

You were in your twenties,

And I was eight years old…

Invisible lines tie me to you

Invisible lines tie me to you whether I like it or not.

No matter how much I travel away from you, no matter how far we are, and no matter how different our roads are;

No matter how distinct our stations are, and no matter how your routes and mine are different;

The invisible lines continue to tie me to you.

Constant they are... they exceed the multitude of people between you and me.

Tense they are...indifferent to the laws of the universe or the gravity of Earth.

Unaffected by the amount of rocks and dismal valleys,

That separate my icy mountain from
your flaming mountain...

(I will continue to love you)

Even if...

Photos these days have become more faithful than people;

Silence in our life has become more eloquent than talking;

And the scent of perfumes can outlast the wearers themselves in places and on hands after greeting each other!

I will continue to love you even if

Eyes has become able to love more than the heart;

The voices of people have got beats, life, and ability to eternally hide in our smart devices more than their owners!

I will continue to love you even if

Conservatives have become these days odd;

Dissidents have become distinguished and civilized;

The fair has become ugly... and the abhorrent has become comfortable;

The sincere have become outcast... and the ambiguous have become needed.

I will continue to love you even if

Scholars have become these days obscure, while licentiousness are celebrities;

Educated people have become rejected and the trivial have become desired.

I will continue to love you even if

Lovers have become rare and Don Juans are too common.

I will continue to L O V E Y O U...

(Hide and seek)

Each of us runs away from the other.

Each of us runs into the other.

Each of us looks for the other.

And each of us knows the hideout of the other...

.

We avoid meeting, yet destiny compels us to meet.

Days separate us, yet people accidentally unite us.

We claim to have forgotten each other, yet we see each other everywhere!

(A broken black umbrella)

Every now and then,

I find myself unintentionally returning to places we once visited together.

Hoping I might find some of me there... and heal from you.

That café at the corner of the street...

I entered it holding a broken black umbrella.

I looked thoroughly at the chairs and stared at the corners.

I went to the wooden round table... the same one that had us around it once.

It was next to the glass overlooking the street.

I ordered a cup of black coffee.

"*Du sucre?*" asked the waiter with a fake smile.

I declined him with a gesture.

I return to my coffee.

I sip it slowly.

Unfamiliar music was playing in the café… I think it was Brazilian.

I finish my coffee…

I pay the cheque.

And I go towards the door of the café.

The waiter runs after me holding my broken black umbrella. I thank him, and leave the place to start my journey of loss…

In Paris city,

And in a world that resembles the unknown,

The faces are similar;

The doors are shut;

And your photos are everywhere!

I see you in the cliché posters displayed on the windows of fashion shops.

I see you in the papers glued on the stands that sell newspapers and magazines in the streets.

I see you in the glossy covers of the international magazines… I see you in the ads of the buses that cross the streets.

I see you in restaurants shops, stations, and doors of the subways. Even some people whom I encounter in the streets suddenly look to me like you or have a resemblance of you.

I wake up from this surrealistic nightmare to find myself have travelled a significant distance from Café de Flor in Saint-Germain until I stopped in the middle of one of the bridges which overlook the seine.

I breathe...

I smile ruefully...

I close my eyes for a while...

I look into the water of the river silently...

I am happy that its water is far from clarity so that I will not see the reflection of your face on it from the nothingness!

I hold my broken black umbrella...

I bid it farewell and confide my memories with you in it forever...

Then I toss it... in the river.

Happy I am because I at last got rid of all feelings I have for you. They drained me those feelings. They were about to drive me crazy in silence.

I leave the place... and everything in it to return to my natural life without you... forever...

On my way to the hotel, a short text-message from you surprises me... after a lifetime!

(Oh stranger)

Oh stranger,

Because of you,

I had to run away... from you!

I, myself, built the barriers and walls between us.

I made them with my hands of my own volition.

Oh stranger,

Because of you,

I, myself, reformed the map of roads.

I made the shiny cities dark,

And made the simple villages dismal.

Oh stranger,

For you,

The traffic lights we gleefully used to wait at them have become gloomy and broken!

The road signs we used to consult to reach our dreams and wishes have become wrecked and unintelligible!

Even the walls of the city we decorated with our colors, wrote our names and initials on them I am about to pull them down.

Oh stranger,

Because of you,

I, myself, built barriers and destroyed bridges.

I destroyed the railroads, so their stations have become deserted and forgotten.

Oh stranger,

Because of you,

I made myself a thousand address

All of which lead of love and forgetfulness.

All of them are available and hidden.

Doors used to close behind us… and now a thousand doors separate us.

On each door, I hung you a mask…

Each hung mask is distinct from the other.

Oh stranger,

Show me now how you will reach me!

And how despite all the painted walls I built

And the forgotten bridges I demolished…

I am certain, as I was one day certain of your love, and running away from you for ages; that these words of mine will somehow find their way to you

And you will know that they were for you

And when you read them, your eyes will water.

Then you will smile and say, "You, mad!"

(A cinematic scene from the past)

It happened that

We were on a pavement at night,

By the river in particular,

Roaring with calamitous laughter.

We jumped together... elegantly dressed... in our heavy wintery clothes into that river!

I knew only then

That remaining with you is a madness-inducing drug...

And distance from you is a death-inducing drug, but slowly...

I had to choose,

And I did.

By the way. I am still keeping the same black coat I was wearing when I was with you that night.

(A default countdown)

I have a problem with losing…

Losing things…

Losing people…

Losing memories…

The losing detail in itself is exhausting for me.

Everything in my life has a meaning and a price.

All things around me have a value. People too have value. Even the sounds I hear or those hiding in my memory do have a value.

Always… whenever I own something new, involuntarily an invisible countdown appears above it.

It counts down like a watch with a low voice. It goes on and on for days and maybe months. It never ceases counting until I lose that thing.

When I lose the thing, it disappears, and so disappears its default countdown with everything related to it forever.

With humans,

At the beginning of any relationship, the default countdown appears. It follows us wherever we go…

I see its beginning, but I do not see its ending…

When I lose them, their default countdown stops counting with the last phone call or meeting...

They disappear, and so does their countdown, but their photos and beautiful stands remain in the mind...even after losing them.

As for love, this issue deserves an Oscar award!

The invisible, default countdown appears and starts counting from moment one.

Its counting is different; its clicks are two times faster being fused with the heartbeats. It counts on and on. I see its beginning, I see its movements, and I see it witnessing our most tender and beautiful moments...

It travels with us, laughs with us, grieves our grief, and dreams with us...

I hear its ending when its time comes because of the explosion of counter when the loss happens. It does not disappear quietly, nor do they disappear with it. Their voices never disappear... only their counter does.

Their images linger and live with me, and their nice stands live in my black box of memories that I will never encounter a more honest one in my life.

To the years of my life that have past, your memories do not deserve to wither; they only deserve to be glowing, lively, and forever throbbing with youth...

(Ships of Memories)

Every night,

The ship of my memories cast their anchors in the ports of the memory

Quietly without any welcoming ceremonies.

Only its flag station in the center.

It slowly flutters;

It has no clear color or writing on it to read.

(If...)

If...

The intentions of people had had voices,

Their internal feelings had had tones,

And their hearts could have uttered the tears it bears!

If...

The minds of people had had voices,

And their eyes codes taught in curricula and teaching courses!

Those who love would have been honest,

And passionate lovers would have lived,

And ardent lovers would have been loyal,

And terrified the dishonest would have been...

After a period of absence

When we met after a period of absence,

I was not myself anymore, nor our meeting was what it used to be.

Not even *Forgetfulness* kept its word when you arrived…

***

Another time

Sometimes I feel as if I do not belong to this time.

I feel I accidentally have fallen from another time…

***

Underneath my skin

You still live in me with all love.

You still live underneath my skin.

You… your memories… and everything that belongs to you.

(Exile)

It happens that writing is sometimes called "Exile" because of the sweet seclusion from others it entails, and the atmosphere it provides that has sculpturing tools only suitable to sculpture a rebellious memory that suffers from a deep hibernation. By the way, I will start writing on you!

***

(A court of law)

This evening I am the defense attorney in the court of law.

My heart is the defendant, and my mind is the judge.

My feelings are the jury and the memories are the eyewitnesses to your love…

***

(Arranging a rendezvous)

Sometimes I arrange our rendezvous that will take place but in the past! I time travel to you from the land of reality to the mazes of memory. I meet you happily and I tell you about everything that happened during your absence.

***

A faculty

Tiring it is to read the faces of people!

Tiring to the reader more than the read.

No matter how difficult people try to hide their feelings or conceal their emotions, there remains a specific person on a specific date who can run into them and read what nobody is entitled to read and see what others cannot see... in others.

***

A box of paint colors

The hearts of people are like a box of paint colors, and the coloring brush is their intentions. Its palette is the environment where people live, and the white board is life. We own the necessary tools to paint that board and fill it with colors that suit what we need.

In the darkness, there is always a spotlight that cannot be seen from anywhere except from within...

A thousand marks

To those who left us, yet their memories, photos, clothes, and the sounds of their laughers remained...

For them remains in the places a thousand marks and in the heart remains a thousand tears...

(A vulture)

I will migrate away from you after a lifetime as a vulture migrates at the age of forty in sight of other birds...

I will break my beak myself so that a new beak that does not know you will grow back.

I will get rid of my talons myself so that new talons that do not know you will grow back.

I will pluck the feathers of my wings myself so that new feathers that do not know you will grow back.

I will become an eagle once again... more powerful and firmer than before... and without you.

***

(...)

I no longer can see clearly whether your love has given me the glow and life or infected me with damage and destruction...

Top Secret...

(**The Rational Love Treaty**)

With reference to the mutual treaty no. 2 dated 18/6 held in Riyadh that contains the terms and conditions of the rational love which maintains that the parties are committed to forget each other forever in case of separation,

We, the Heart, would like to inform you of the necessity of adhering to the compelling condition in the treaty between the two parties in order to avoid severing the remaining memory relationships between us. It has been noticed lately many reckless, uncalculated movements from your side. We hereby hope you control yourself and think more wisely.

The Heart would also like to seize this opportunity to inform you that it has never forgot you, and it still beats, smiles, and grieves silently each time it hears news about you.

For your notice and information...

best wishes

Signature:
Director of the Memory Section in the Heart

Sometimes we think that we are in love with someone. However, we are actually in love with the state that we only lived with them.

A grey train station

Its color is grey... that station located between remoteness and nearness. Passengers always do not notice it at the beginning of their journeys.

The station of silent language... the station of decisions... the station of beholding things clearly. It is a station that you buy from the seller at the stand a cup of coffee, a piece of paper and a pencil to draw for yourself a correct roadmap. You either continue the journey with your companion or end the journey peacefully and simply return to the first station.

To take a decision and return alone courageously and confidently from the grey station to the point of beginning is much better than continuing a journey on a misleading, ambiguous roadmap that may someday lead you to the wrong station – "The Black Devastating Station."

A dagger of gold

I gave you my heart as a present with its keys, its boxes of secrets, its loyalty, and all its attention.

And you gave me a dagger of gold as a present. It was the single one in the world that has no second. The word "loyalty" was engraved on it then you stabbed me with it!

I gifted you with the lifetime that was, the lifetime that will be, and the lifetime that has not happened, yet. You gifted me with a lost lifetime whose beginning cannot be distinguished from its ending... life time of undated days and uneven nights.

(I am no longer)

I am no longer able to find any excuses for you, or for your actions, and contradictory words...

I am no longer able to see things as I used to do with you!

Let me be more specific; because of you, I am no longer myself as I was previously.

Something inside me froze, and I do not see anything special in you anymore.

A destroyed village

You are asking me how I am doing after you!

Like asking a village how it is doing after someone caused its destruction and left it!

After you,

My blood become ashes, and all my artillery ammunition of love ran out.

I hereby declare my defeat before your absence and inform you that you can depart forever...

My feelings to you

You are asking me about my feelings for you!

My feelings for you are cast of gold; gold never rusts or wears out no matter how long it takes.

But you know that gold can be melted and recast in different shapes.

The big question is, "Do you have the ability to comprehend these casts and save them in a safe place not to be stolen from you one day?"

***

Pride

Moodiness has always been a barrier between you and me.

I refuse to give my pride up, and you refuse the idea of separation!

I stand at the edge of the world, while you are in its center.

Each of us is silently looking at the other from our places as if time has stopped!

Platform of station no. 1

On the platform of station no. 1 while waiting the long-awaited train, I began recalling all my memories with you as flashes.

Flashes… flashes… flashes… places and dates… faces and reverberating photos of us together… sounds and stands… your promises jump from my memory before my own eyes on the platform as rabbits jump from the hat of the magician before the audience… I saw with my eyes the dreams that we once built together evaporating and rising like the fumes of factories in the outskirts of the city.

I then become certain – it was too too late – that love on its own is not sufficient.

While I was standing on platform no. 1, the train arrived. Before I enter the car, I was wondering whether my decision to break up with you would be correct later or I would regret it one day in the future.

I reached a conclusion that regretting taking a reaction that might be wrong in the future is much better and way easier for me than regretting not taking any decision or reaction regarding what I feel now.

On the platform of station no. 1, in front of the train, I waited for you.

You did not come, so I left.

***

A box of matches

Your promises for me are like matches organized in a box of matches. Each day you light me one match and the box is about to run out.

(A sarcastic conversation)

A: I love you as big as the sea, with all its waves, the depth of its blueness and the lengths of its shores.

B: And I love you too... like a fish which is still alive in that sea. It lives in the depth of its heart and knows that "it is not the only one there!"

(Someday)

Someday I will leave you forever.

I will depart you. I will leave the places that had us together one day. I will leave the dreams we built together out of nowhere. I will leave from your name.

I will leave from you voice, your wardrobe, your perfume, your book placed on the shelf, your watch, your cracked cup of coffee, and your terrace that our elderly neighbor used to lean out of her window to greet us and tell us about the weather.

I will leave both of us.

I will emit your breath cherished in my breast, and then I will leave from myself because of you.

Every now and then

A live photo of you storms into me every now and then for five seconds only.

A live photo of you storms into me without a prior notice indifferent to time or place. It can because of a scent of perfume like yours in a public place, a sentence similar to your way of speaking somebody uttered accidentally, a painting at the entrance of a hotel, a piece of music, rain, clouds, Charriol, Natalie Portman, December, or instant coffee.

For five seconds only, I meet you face to face every now and then.

(Platform of station no. 2)

I told you I was leaving.

I told you I was no longer able to continue in that the midair state between earth and the sky.

Its beginning was clear, its medium stage is ambiguous, and its ending is unknown!

I told you that I would wait for you for the last time before I leave.

On platform of station no. 2, I waited for you.

You came, but I left.

(Separation is the solution)

When we get to that level of tiring love, separation
is the solution.

When meeting is painful and exhausting this much,
and jealously embodies the shape of love, separation
is the solution.

When the relationship is merely taking attendance and taking
leave while each of us intentionally keep themselves busy from
the other, separation is the solution.

When you suddenly shed a tear in a public place and the
internal dialogue of the mind comes to the stage of "Am I
staying with you because I love you or because I fear change?"
separation is the solution.

(Gratitude)

I am grateful to the days that crossed out paths.

I am grateful to the conditions and causes that contributed to arranging meeting you.

I am grateful to all of the moments we spent together that are still stored and throbbing with life until now in my memory.

I am grateful to all cups of coffee we sipped together.

I am grateful to the insomnia that the coffee we drank together caused to us.

I am grateful to the streets, to the places, to the songs that accompanied us in our days, and to the people who supported us, always loved to see us together, and spared us no one bit of advice or a gentle, supporting word. I am grateful to the life, cities, and air.

Here we are... we have separated and each of us lives in a country, so I am grateful to the memories that I had with you.

I have never forgot you since we broke up, and I know that you have never forgot me for one moment.

***

(A Star)

Each star in the sky was previously a tear of a lover in the past. It froze over time, transformed into a shining crystal until the Milky Way saw it from afar, and added it to its constellation after it had settled in the sky.

Each star in the sky stores some story of some person in some time.

(A leaked telegram)

Where are you?

I lost contact with your voice.

Your voice is still in my memory.

It was always insistent.

It was blazing with love, longing, and youth.

Where are you?

I lost contact with your news.

Your news was ever new and full of crazy stories and events.

It has always made me laugh.

Our mutual friends who used to provide me with intermittent bits of news about you have disappeared and are no longer inhabitant of this city.

I do not actually know whether your disappearance was intentional or unintentional.

All I know is that you still live in my mind. You leave for a while then I suddenly find you throbbing in my blood.

(Platform of station no. 3)

Running away.

I am still running away from you

I am still running away from the eluding justice of your heart.

The authorities of your heart tried hard to capture me.

They could not do it.

I glanced you arguing with the conductor from afar.

I do not know whether I actually saw you or I imagined I did!

On the platform of station no. 3, I did not wait you, and you did not come, so I left.

(A small music box)

You are still present in my mind.

Your elegant soul still hovers above my head like a cloud.

Your photo is still stuck on the wall of my memories like a balloon of helium sticks to the ceiling of a room.

Your voice is still for me like a piece of music.

I listen to it like somebody listening to favored musical notes of a small music box.

He never stops rotating the handle until he can no longer resist drowsiness, so he falls asleep to the sound of the music.

(Platform of station no. 4)

The train has stopped.

All passengers started to take off.

I look at them quietly with awe and worry.

I am on my own now.

On my own!

without you!

For the first time since some time, I have a strange feeling now.

Conflicting feelings...

I have forgot how to be on my own.

I have lost most of the skills and tools I had previously to be able to live on my own.

I am on my own again!

Am I really ready?

Am I really ready to begin anew?

Will I see the things around with their beautiful colors anew?

Will the damaged part of my heart heal?

Will I forget?

Will I be able to love anew?

Will I meet someone able to make me love anew?

The door of the train car ahead of me stands between me and the beginning of my new life without you, your memory and everything related to you.

If I cross it, I will survive from you for good.

On the platform of station no. 4, I did not cross the door of the car; rather, I vigorously jumped away from it.

I am sick of crossword puzzles with you!

I may have wronged you

When I intend to not reproach you or try to avoid seeing what you wrong me, it does not mean I did not notice it or I am a tough person void of feelings or proof to his surroundings. It actually means that I am determined to see all good in you and that I still believe you will be better over time.

With you, I endeavor to find a thousand excuses for you because someday because of you I will leave you for good. I do not need then to feel that I may have wronged you.

***

Optional silence

With you, I am silent all the time not because I am not skilled at talking or do not know anything to talk about; rather, it is because I love you and I need to avoid any conversation with you that may lead to losing you, or you losing yourself.

Enquiry

Enquiry is always the beginning of doubt, so I will not enquire whether I still see you with that pure, beautiful image I used to have for you in the past.

***

Go away... so I see you clearly

I no longer can see things around me as I used to in the past.

Go away!

I no longer can see you as I used to see you before when you are close to me.

I do not know whether I still love you more or hate you more.

All I know now is that I need you to move far away until I can see you and see things clearly in their real shape once again.

(Leaving you is the solution)

It suffices me that I knew you once and loved you without limits, boundaries or even traditions.

I suffices me that I lived with you like a free bird infatuated with flying between the ground and the sky knowing well that falling is an inevitable evil.

I never regretted any decision I took with you because your love taught me that if wounded, leaving you is the solution.

***

(I will change my addresses)

I will get rid of my thoughts plagued with you.

I will shun my feelings addicted to you.

I will change my addresses.

I will empty my lungs of the air that belongs to you.

Then I will live free again.

A empty quarter

There is a empty quarter in my heart that has not been damaged, yet.

No human heard of it and no days knew of it.

It has never been moved by an emotion or touched by separation.

There is a empty quarter in my heart waiting tomorrow with hope and a promise.

***

A telegram

Where were you when the sun left our – your and my – sweet memories ?

Where were you when the sun was absent from our beautiful memories , you and I?

(I have decided to)

Love needs power and efforts and I have exhausted all my power and efforts with you!

I have decided to live without you and without your love.

I have decided to live a different love—a unique love.

I have decided to love the things around me.

I have decided to love the things I already had which I forgot because I was busy loving you.

I have decided to concern myself with loving the people who had been in my life before you entered it.

I have decided to love life, to love hope, to love the future, to love the sky, to look thoroughly at the sky.

I have decided to love myself that I neglected because paying close attention to you kept me away from it.

Love needs power and efforts.

And loving you needs forgetfulness and to start anew.

You used to ask me for days, months, and years to respond to you with at least a word.

Here I am today; I am responding to you by a book!

On the way to you

I look at the buildings in the streets from the car window on the way to you. I contemplate their lights, quietness, and steadiness, so I smile. I had an idea then; what if both of us transformed into two quiet, stable buildings adjacent to each other forever?

***

Reciprocity

I cannot deal with you on the basis of the principle of reciprocity. You will hate me if I do. If was insignificant to you, you will never be insignificant to me!

(Unreadable)

Do not try to read me. You won't be able to do it.

How can you read a thousand men living in one body?

Do not try to confine me. You won't be able to do it.

How do you confine a bird whose shelter is the sky and joy is to fly in it.

Have you ever heard of a bird that had been confined in a cage and could live?

Do not try to outsmart me. You won't be able to do it.

I have a hat like a magician that will usher you into mazes with yourself. It has a beginning without an ending.

Do not try to categorize me. You won't be able to do it.

I am as changeable and varied as the seasons of the year are. In each season, I will appear to you in a new shape, new color, and newer presence.

Do not try to formulate me. You won't be able to do it.

I am air-like. Can you shape wind?

Instead of all of that, just try to win me as I am if I really mean something for you and you care for me because at the beginning with you, I tried with you just to win you.

***

(The public library of the city)

One day,

You will happen to look for me everywhere;

You will annoy our mutual friends with
your indirect questions;

You will search in the public library of the city;

You will go through its shelves one by one;

You will annoy the visitors and the librarian will expel you.

You will leave the place desperate and decide to forget me.

Just before you reach your home, you will find somebody
reminding you of me in a poster on your way.

Love does not knock doors to enter;

Love is a silent thief feared and loved by all simultaneously.

Things that were said

All things that were said, are being said, and will be said are nothing more than representation of internal reflections of the personality of the speaker.

We also win other people with an honest word coming from the heart, and we lose them with an in appropriate word.

***

The lion's share

Life always takes me to the unexpected!

And chances always have the lion's share in love.

(You will lose)

Life is very short.

If you will live it according to the points of view of other people, you will lose.

Other people are changeable, so are their views.

(Rules of love)

There is no one specific, successful rule in love.

There is no clear roadmap in it.

Each case has its own special symptoms and complications. There is no idealism in love nor is there order. Love is chaotic and cannot be planned for.

Each love has its own heroes, its own conditions, its own timing, its own scenario, conversation and special scenes.

Love is live like your daily bread.

It looks for you... you do not look for it.

It follows you wherever you are, and you cannot escape it.

Every human

Every human has their special concept of love and special way to deal with it according to their social background and the conditions of their upbringing, ideas… and luck!

***

A surprise guest

Love is like a surprise guest.

It knocks your door without a prior call, text message, or a prior notice.

You either receive it at that moment with due respect, or at least let it pass with dignity to another person who can receive it duly.

A means to avenge themselves

We cannot apply the experiences of other people in love.

We are the only ones who are capable of determining the circumstances of each relationship we involve ourselves in.

They will endeavor, out of love without paying any attention, to choose our new experience as a means to avenge themselves for a previous love experience they failed in.

***

Aristotle and Al-Nabigha

Had people been affected with other people's experiences and rules of love in history, educated people would have learned from the books of Aristotle and Plato on love or from the seven Mu'allaqat poetry masterpieces on love by Al-Nabigha and Imru' al-Qais.

People learn only from their own experiences.

(Concise scale)

In all love relationship we get ourselves in, we are its concise scale, the true indicator of the relationship and its dimensions.

It is illogical to seek the advice of other people, and then blame them when it fails.

***

(Permanent damage)

It is comforting that never before has anyone dies of love, but it happened that they were permanently damaged because of it.

***

(The end does not justify the means)

In love, the end does not justify the means. You cannot lock up a butterfly in a bottle because you are afraid it might be burned by light. It will die.

A fugitive from love

Some people fear love. They avoid all roads that might lead to it, fight it, keep distance from it, and run away from it like a prey running away from the wild beasts. Despite of that, they accidentally fall in love and they happen to feel happy in it.

***

The best in you

Those who love you change you for the better.

They invoke the best in you. They take care of you, develop you, and adhere to you.

Those who love you, you will be their present day, you will be their yesterday, and you will be their tomorrow.

Their endless passion will be to remain with you.

(You flaws before your merits)

Those who love you will love your flaws before your merits.

They will fall in love with everything connected to you or belongs to you.

They will try to understand your points of view, see what you perceive and what suits you despite disagreeing with you.

They will be happy for your happiness. They will comfort you in your sadness. They will tell you tomorrow will be better, and they will not desert you when all people do.

Whereas those who hate you will not see in you, or in what you offer, anything they like or favor.

They will just endeavor to look for flaws or defects in you to shed light on them in order to get themselves busy and occupy you in yourself. If you responded to them, you will be giving them importance they do not actually deserve. This kind of people has become flagrant these days. Other people can see it clearly no matter how many means, masks, or ways it has.

The truest love

The mother's love is the truest and most secure love in life.

Any other love is just a drop in the sea.

The mother's love is the most precious and the most lasting love over time.

Compared to it, the failure of any love in life becomes easier.

***

A sharp instrument

In the law of true love, honesty becomes a sharp instrument that continuously stabs the heart of the honest party in the relationship at the "moment of separation".

Love in the wilderness

You cannot search for love in the wilderness like looking for a game in a hunting journey.

Love is an attitude. Love is a word. Love is loyalty.

Love is giving.

Love is not a pronoun that indicates absence;

It is an adverb of motion and time.

Love is for the pure who arm themselves with forgiveness while in the state of power. Forgiveness is a merit that belongs to them only.

Your true image

People who try to find their true image in the eyes of humans or in the reflections of mirrors are like those trying to lay the foundations of a house on a surface of quicksand. Each time they complete the building, they feel happy and proud of their achievement. The following morning, a shock of betrayal strikes them when they find that the sand, aided by the wind and its currents, has shifted, changed and buried most of the building.

Our real images are revealed when we are on our own; they appear as a reflection in the eyes of the people in our lives. They love us as we are and know us well away from the eyes of other people and their changing standards.

Act out of the league but loyally

Being unique from the league does not mean you do not belong to it; it means that you need to be distinguished with something different and new that might yield success and excellence for you and the group in the near future. Act out of the league but loyally.

***

An explanation

The hours of your day are more important than wasting them explaining to other people the reasons of your actions.

Other people are actually who need to find a way to understand you if they really care for you.

Changeable and unpredictable

In this life, we do not need to convince other people of what we have. Humans are changeable and unpredictable.

We need to improve and strengthen out tolerance skills to maintain our ideas, principles, and goals for the future. Those who criticize you initially will clap their hands for you when you succeed.

***

Company

How beautiful it is when God blesses you with people honest with you and themselves, who love you and know well your details, whom you trust, whom you enjoy their presence, whom you feel happy to meet, and whom you are proud because they inhabit the map of your life! They are, for you, are more than just company.

A telescope lense

Take a closer look at the simple things you have, rub them a little and try to look at them through the lense of a telescope. Look for the aspects of beauty in them; you will find that God has already granted you more than what you actually need.

***

An analysis

Me... you... them...

Each of us sees things from our own perspective. All ways are correct, but the difference between me, you, and them us the way of analyzing these things.

(Purity)

Purity is not a characteristic of the things around us or a quality we look for in others; purity lodges in our ideas and our souls. It exists in our eyes and the way of conceiving things, people around us, and our way of analyzing them and their actions.

***

(It happens)

It happens that the events of your past life flash before you like screenshots of a silent movie. You see your stands towards yourself, and then your stands with the people closest to you.

It is...

It is the beginning of every good and the key of all earnings...
It is a bless for everyone who has it. Those who enjoy it will
not be able to live without it in their life because of its beauty
and the beauty that yields from it. It is the "good intention."

***

Inferiority

Your sense of inferiority is a feeling particular to you only. Do
not accuse other people and harm them with it; they are not
liable for your feelings or the psychological fluctuations and
complexes in your mind.

***

Do you have an idea?

You have no idea about the obstacles and barriers all successful
people crossed in their lives to reach their successes. Humans
care only for the last stage of anything.

(*Nouveau Riche*)

If you need to discover *Nouveau Riche* people as soon as possible, watch their behavior, conversation style, etiquette, respect to themselves first and then to other people around them. Do not look at the amount of money they spend on the labels of their watches and the frequency of their travels each year.

***

(No escape...)

There is no escape from the past because it lives in us and we are saturated with it.

There is no escape from the present because it lives in us, and we still live in it.

What about the future?

(Be yourself)

To live, you have two options:

You either live fragile without a personality occupying yourself with the views of people trying to formulate yourself as it suits them, their lives, and their changing standards over time. They themselves most probably do not apply!

Or you be yourself, so you win yourself; you accept your points of weaknesses, attempt to overcome them, have a good command over your strengths, enjoy the ability to endure the price of your difference and distinction from others, and convinced of the constant standards that you, yourself, see suitable for yourself and your life.

They hate you at the beginning not because of anything in yourself; people usually hate those different from them. They consider that being different from them is a form of rebellion.

Do not worry. Over time when you reach your goal and succeed, they will accept you then they will love you. They will see the good in you and respect the strength of your faith and resilience to reach your goal. They are in the first place humans like you. Humans err; they can be like you or better than you. However, their fear of change or taking initiatives has created a kind of rejection to make changes and others making changes.

The dream materializes if we need that with determination, and illusion becomes an illness if it went too far without curbing it.

***

(Addiction)

Ant sane person may get addicted to anything without awareness or knowledge of them.

It happens, for example, that we get addicted to the voices of those we love unintentionally.

***

(Nobody is lucky)

Nobody is lucky in everything, and nobody possesses everything. Luck plays its role at the beginning only. What remains is your efforts and God's assistance.

Not in them

It happens that people may see in others what is not in them. At the end, humans see what they need to see. They see only what they think of.

***

A feeling of rejection

Some people cannot coexist with the others' feeling of rejection. You discover after it is too late that the main drive behind their offensive behavior towards you is their not accepting your insistence to maintain a distance between you and them. You consider it a private space, but they consider it rejection for them; thus, they offend you.

(I am neither a friend for all... neither do I aspire to)

I am neither a friend for all, neither do I aspire to.

What I care for is to stay in good terms with all people, and maintain the few friends I have in my life. They are my true friends who time proved their good stands and different places documented their noble deeds. It is not necessary to describe your good relationship with other people as friendship; it is not important to be friends with your colleagues at work or be surrounded by a battalion of friends.

It is rare that people have real friends, if it happens, they will be few, and it is stupid to easily lose them. Friendship has its conditions, terms, and responsibilities. One either performs them correctly or distances themselves not to do injustice to the concept of friendship. The most important and safest thing for friendship is to maintain a good relationship with all people without coming too close, going further or raising expectations. Look at all people as they are really not as you wish them to be in order to not be shocked because of them in the future or in reality.

(Bullying)

Most people who suffered from verbal bullying during their study levels because of their appearance, color, voice, race, gender, shyness, difference, weakness, physical body structure, simplicity of their dress, poorness, orphanhood, high grade point average, isolation, various hobbies, low efficiency at vandalism, surnames, or even their social class, have become later of the most successful and efficient in their societies.

***

(Strong)

Only the strong can distinguish between respect and weakness, between strength and injustice, and between love and possessing...

Exhausting are those minute details that never departed the harbors of the memory!

(86 billion of marginalized neurons)

The brain consists of 86 billion neurons. Each neuron sends and receives electromagnetics signals to thousands others neurons. The stock of memories, words, emotions, feelings, and mental capabilities occupies the biggest portion of these neurons. So do not claim, dear, that you are able to feel other people and things around you. Your intentional ignoring and marginalizing that massive amount of the sensory cells that inhabit you, that God has bestowed on you, indicates that there is a defect or a problem in your nervous system.

(Unreal)

All talks and stories which exchanged and discussed with friends or other people in café, gyms, restaurants, meetings, or even work are mostly unreal governed by showing off or idealism.

True talks are those ones stripped from any masks or falsehood, such as conversations that happen on the plane with a stranger, when you both don't know your each other's real name. Also, you both know that your meeting in the air will be the first and last one.

***

(Caffeine)

Paying too much attention to the details of your relationship with the person whom you love is going to ruin it. Try to see what will help to develop the relationship, improves its quality, and increases its glow; try to find points of convergence between you. If one of you likes, for instance, coffee and the other likes tea, you can look at the positive side; you both like caffeine!

Strict Rules

Sometimes we feel happy when some people enter our lives without any prior introductions. We feel happy for their awesome insistence to enter it.

Because of them, we find ourselves obliged to give up the strict rules we laid and observed with other people.

***

A white swan

Today I accidentally met a white swan so fair and elegant. It was waiting in the city pond on its own unaware of what destiny holds for it. Its waiting may end in one moment and it might last for years and years. Only the Omniscient knows.

A noisy village

You always confuse yourself trying to categorize me. You once array me the dress of quietness and another time the dress of noisiness.

I am, dear, a mixture of the quietness of villages and the nosiness of cities. I cannot take one side rather than the other. A part of me resides here and another dwells there.

***

Silence

By silence, we can narrate what words fail to deliver.

By silence, we can accomplish what only God knows.

***

I know you know

I know you know that I always read everything that goes in your mind, and I know also that you endeavor to convince me otherwise...

How beautiful it is that your relationship with some people begins with a coincidence, and then you end up in love!

A look inadvertently omitted

Everything you feel or sense reaches me no matter how much you try to conceal it. I see you as clearly as I see the sun.

***

To be or not to be

Do not force me to choose whether to be for you imminently or never be yours. My calmness before your overwhelming, kind emotions does not mean I am not interested or appreciative; it means that I have studied you quietly. I am trying not to take any other step ahead with you until I make sure of you, who you really are, the extent of your patience, the limits of your emotions, how you care, and my status in your heart because I do not need to repeat the same mistakes I did in the past. They would make us weary of each other.

A rehearsal

You do not have to memorize a page of a literary book to come back and perform it before me to impress me as if you are in a rehearsal.

Let things develop naturally, and do not forget that there is an art for memorization and an art for performing as well as an art for feeling. The beauty of feeling lies in its genuineness. Otherwise, professional, experienced theatre actors would not have fallen in love with each other in sight of the audience despite their awareness and cautiousness due to a moment of genuineness among them. They believed in it, surrendered to it, and refused to give it up.

***

Without barriers

The speech of your heart and its beats reaches me without any barriers...

Your looks, smiles, questions, interest wrapped in pride, frowning during conversations, silence, glances when people are busy, presence, absence, promises, happiness, comic side, and concealing your sadness reach me all. I read you silently.

A tear inadvertently remained

Feeling your pain is sufficient to make the world
cry this evening.

In the hospital behind the glass, I watch you silently while you
are in pain. Had I been able to suffer the pain instead of you,
I would have done it.

I laugh and wave for you as an attempt to simplify the situation.
You look at me, endure your pain, smile, and claim it is not
that bad. You do not know that a tear inadvertently remained
between your eyelids. You have forgot to wipe it away as you
have forgot that I see things around me as they are clearly. I
would like to tell you that this heavy evening with all it contains
shall come to an end and tomorrow will be more beautiful.

You will see it.

How can you not see that when you are the most precious
person in the world?

***

Many options

I know that I had, and still have, many options, yet I have
chosen you. My heart will never ceases choosing you to be the
only and the lasting person who dwells in it.

***

Graffiti

The feelings I have for you in my heart cannot be simply
unloaded in the air, on paper, as literary works, or symbols or
graffiti written by paint sprayers on walls to decorate them. The
thing is bigger, closer, further, simpler, and far more complicated.

***

I cannot

I cannot tell them about you.

I cannot tell them that my life with you has become more beautiful, and it is not as it had been before you.

I only can conceal you from them in the depth of my heart to protect you.

***

A confession

I confess to you that I need your existence in my life.

Your existence helps me to go on. It helps me to be better.

Butterflies' love

I love you as butterflies love light. They hover around it happily knowing well that it will burn them up, and they will die because of it any minute.

***

Optional solitude

Optional solitude…

A safe heaven I resort to and hide from other people with my scattered manuscripts everywhere, incomplete paintings, books, memories… and most importantly with you.

***

I do not care

You accuse me that I do not pay attention or care, while I freeze for long hours in front of papers when I decide to write about you. I do not know where to start from and where to get off the enormity of what is in in my heart for you.

You look at me with eyes like an inkwell. I resort to their help to write for you or write about you.

A meeting in the virtual world

I have worn the suitable glasses and laid sheets of paper on the desk to write about you when I am back.

I went to look for you in the virtual world; I met you there, and since then I never returned.

***

A rendezvous

I have a rendezvous with you each night in my memories. I watch your smile for a while and look thoroughly in your eyes for another. Then I fall asleep to your voice.

(A dream)

Since we always dream of what we think about, I am going to think about you each day, hour, minute, and second. Then I will meet you in my dream.

***

(Telepathy)

It always surprises me when you occur to me without any prior notice.

I do not know if this is a kind of telepathy or just feeling you from afar.

On board of a cloud

Ideas always carry my outsides the bounds of the place. I travel on board of a cloud whose fuel is a sigh and destination is waking up from a dream.

***

An empty bottle of perfume

An empty bottle of perfume can invoke an unexpected state of nostalgia that causes you to travel mentally to far places you have not seen for ages, nor do you have any knowledge about the people who were with you there back then. You smile and curiosity comes over you for a while.

(An alien)

A stranger told me once that we were no longer living on the planet of love and the latest people who used to love genuinely left for good in the 1970s. They all migrated to Mars and no longer inhabit this planet.

I do not know why I cautiously smiled and felt for a moment that I was an alien!

***

(I write for you)

I write for you words and symbols everywhere... on stones as hieroglyphics, on the back of school gates and electricity pillars, and on cafés napkins so you may use them on your way to reach me.

A transparent star

In public places with passers-by in the middle of the crowds and in the faces of the people, I always see you as a transparent star shining from afar.

***

A city without a name

I dream of a faraway city without a name, boundaries, and people – a city only inhabited by you and me.

***

Memory of fish

It is said that the span of the memory of fish renews every seven seconds! Some scientists have recently discovered that some species of fish can remember events for two weeks!

I wish I were able to replace my love memory with the memory of fish whose span renews every seven seconds!

I contribute to your leaving and support your distance, while you always insist on returning and remaining!

Love in a moment of weakness

I cannot love you now. I cannot make sure whether I am able to I love you or not. I oppose decisions taken in moments of weaknesses. I cannot make decisions; your love seems more than awesome, but I have not done yet with previous feelings that are still dwelling in me.

***

Silverware signed by celebrities

Oh stranger,

You do not have to roll out red carpets and light candles in your palace to impress me.

You do not have to show the best you have of silverware signed by celebrities to grab my attention.

In a simple, passing moment of honesty, you can possess my heart and everything in it.

The most difficult places

Stop using conditions as excuses. Stop taking distances as excuses.

True love dwells in the most difficult places. It continues through tough roads and stations. It shines in the most difficult situations and places. It does not wait for any time and place preparations.

***

I tried

I, the undersigned, hereby acknowledge and confess that one day I tried hard to love you and see you in a similar way to the one you used to see me, but I did not succeed.

I apologize to you and to my soul that was strained because of that attempt.

(I refuse to refuse)

Do not ask me to retire from the world or to drop out of sight because of I love you very much.

Do not try to restrain me with golden handcuffs,
and then convince me of their beauty when they are
confining my hands!

Do not imprison me in your breast until I suffocate, and then ask me to breathe!

Do not burry me dreams alive fearing I may leave you one day, and then ask me to smile!

Do not hold me accountable for the reactions of other people around me, and then shed light on their flaws to make yourself stand out!

I know who you are, and I know the space I have in the map of your heart. I know also that you have enough awareness to know that you do not have to cancel my existence or rationalize my attention fearing that I may leave you.

It will destroy you

Begging for emotions from the person whom you love will not advance your relationship with them; it will destroy the relationship, and then it will destroy you because in the law of love, the things people request either die out or lose their value forever.

***

Your stunning performance does not impress me any more

I do not belong to anything except life... love...and giving.

I do not belong to your changing words, false promises, or performance that is similar to a stunning performance of a magician... three-thirds of which is tricks and the remaining fourth is an illusion !

Human copies

I do not like human copies in love even if they are impressive copies with more emotions. I prefer the original one and perceive their merits even if they are limited or simple. The original for me is more honest and lasting.

With you...

My feeling guides me with people and things around me. My feelings are what guides me to what is always unexpected and to the furthest point ever even with you.

***

Thank you...

Thank you!

You have changed my life to the better. I have become able to see things easier because of you, and I see you more beautiful when you are far.

It happens that you take a surprise step without prior preparation, and it becomes the best and most successful decision in your life!

(A black tie)

Who said black is a bleak color?

Coffee is black, yet we drink it in the most important joyous celebrations!

The same is true for black ties. They are not always a sign of bad mood, a sad occasion, or depression; they might refer to classism, mysteriousness, and lacking interest to draw attention.

Black is the only color in the world capable to coexist and preserve its elegance even in the bleakest situations.

Your historic heritage

The historic heritage of your family and their glory matters to you only and does not interest other people. You are entitled to be proud of it to certain extents without undervaluing other people and without letting arrogance carry you away. It is a trust put with you that you should add up to it rather than consuming it. You have to protect it, represent it properly, and hand it over like a badge of honor to the coming generation without tarnishing it.

We love them from afar but...

Sometimes we see people from afar and find them impressing, so we love them, care for them, fall in love with their details, tell others about them, try to be like them, and dream to meet them accidentally someday. We compose thousands of scenarios in our imagination to arrange that meeting. Days pass by and fate brings us accidentally with them; we draw ourselves closer to them and they shock us!

We feel disappointed; it shocks us that they are in reality completely different. We discover that we loved the imagined version of them that we created for them in our imagination from afar.

They are beautiful from afar, they are honest from afar, they are simple from afar, they are loyal from afar, and they are loving from afar.

They love to show off that they love

Some people love to show off that they love. Their fear of being alone confuses them. The sounds of their friends and their conversations about love annoy them. They simply do not need to be less than their friends.

***

My moments with you

Precious are my moments with you, and I do not find it necessary to tell you. You are one of those people who cannot continue giving if they know of a person's love to them; I have decided not to tell you in order to keep you are as you are – loving and always giving.

I write about you...not to make you come back; I actually need to get rid of the things that used to upset me, but I couldn't tell you about them back then.

You are late

Had our meeting today taken place at its correct timing years from now, it would have been different!

Had you said what you spoke today years from now, it would have been different.

I am sorry. I am not available today.

All the feelings I had had for you have become just wishes that you succeed in your life.

Traveller coffee

My traveller coffee is so loyal to me. It accompanies me wherever I go in this world.

I wander in the streets of different cities and capital cities holding it in my hand. It never got bored or tired.

It witnessed all moment of happiness I had.

It felt sad for the disappointments that affected me.

My traveller coffee…

I love it black without any additives because, maybe, I always prefer to fall in love with the original things as they really are without any additions or modifications.

(Slowly)

I walk slowly holding in my hand my happiness and
the journey's precautions.

I walk slowly heading to my wishes with those people in my
life on bare feet and a quarter of a heart.

***

(A loyal friend)

Because I am a friend loyal to places, I carefully pick the
places I visit.

And because I am a friend loyal to memories, I pick the
memory that hurts me the most.

(My lighthouse friend)

You have always been there for me in the bleakest moments…

You have always accepted me and respected me as I am not as you want…

You have always listened to my long talks—the serious and silly ones as well…

You have always witnessed the most important stages and turning points in my life…

I have always leaned on you in the most important stations in life…

You have always guided me to the correct route to anchor in the correct harbor as lighthouses guide sailors and direct them to the correct rout.

The situations have changed, life did as well, and people changed over time, yet you did not.

I am deeply grateful to the strange coincidence that brought us together.

I am proud of you and of your friendship.

I am also thankful to you, my lighthouse friend!

A damage in the phone receiver

I still remember the last phone call between us; I was listening to you quietly. The amount of false justification in that call was sufficient to make the receiver in my hand shout out!

I still also remember my too late conclusion that words in my world have meanings and conjugations different from those in your world.

I remember then that I hung up the receiver violently; I caused a permanent damage to its base and to my heart later.

On that day, everything between us ended.

(Clothes)

Confusing and terrifying are those who have the ability to see what is inside you clearly while the whole world is occupied with your smile, clothes, and presence you have exhibited.

***

(Free fall)

The last moment of love that belonged to you has fallen from my heart the same as the last autumn leaf has fallen from a tree branch.

Cities in which I see what I need to see only.

(Paris)

Charles de Gaulle Airport

...

Concorde La Fayette

...

A broken black umbrella

...

Le Monde

...

Café George V

...

Saint-Germain

...

Eiffel Tower

...

Seine river

...

Black coffee

...

Alain Delon

...

Parole... parole... parole

The city of elegance…

The city of beauty…

The city of tender skins and expensive fur…

Concorde La Fayette city

The city of love and no limits…

The city of the rational and irrational…

The city of rebelling against logic…

The city whose inhabitants eat cheese at the end of meals!

An ancient city disguising in the body of a young woman…

The only city in the world that has the ability to shift from romanticism to drama in one second.

The only city in the world that that has the ability to contribute to providing an incredible surrealistic as well as tragic atmosphere in one moment because, maybe, it is the city that witnessed most of the disappointments of lovers from all around the world over time.

It is a city with a fresh face and another one as pale as separation.

I know the latter face very well.

(**Tokyo**)

Night

…

Silence

…

Lights of the city

…

Quietness

…

Close buildings

…

Order

…

Motion

…

Crossroads

…

Police

…

Clean taxis

…

Crowds of people

…

Elegance

...

Peculiar etiquette

...

Kimonos

...

Honesty

...

High quality

...

Excessive respect

...

Art

...

History

...

Innovation

...

Contemplation

...

It is a city whose people believe in natural beauty in everything.

It is a city whose inhabitants are some of the most elegant people in the world if they are not the best indeed!

It is a city whose inhabitants fall in love with highly animated cartoon characters!

When you walk around Tokyo at night jumping from one pavement to the other, it feels like entering a virtual world. The only difference is that it is real.

It is the only city in the world where you feel when you visit it that you are in another planet different from Earth.

The streets are different, the buildings are different, the etiquette is different, the humans are different, and even time is different and fast.

It is a city where you can view the past, the present, and the future at the same moment.

(Beirut)

Al Ramla Al Baida

…

Raouché

…

Ashrafieh

…

Beirut café

…

Julia Boutros songs

…

Em Sherif Resturant

…

Ras Beirut

…

Riad Al Solh Square

…

Adjacent mosques and churches

…

Historic coexistence

…

Al Falamanki

…

Martyrs Square

…

Al Mandaloun café

…

Dbayeh

It is the city of harmony and beauty.

It is the city of sects and religions.

It is a city whose inhabitants love life.

It is a city whose inhabitants look like the world.

It is a city whose inhabitants are creative in hospitality.

It is a city celebrities and the laypeople sit in the same restaurant without the latter violating the privacy of the earlier even with a look.

(**Riyadh**)

The capital city

...

1990s

...

House no. 1

...

Residents of the neighborhood

...

Caps trimmed in gold

...

A sole tree at the entrance of the house

...

The Officers' Club

...

Happy final exams

...

Saudi Arabian Airlines

...

Al Riyadh Newspaper

...

Rawdat Khuraim

...

Najd

...

Instant camera

...

Marhaba grocery

...

Mamaz neighborhood

...

Gazzaz

...

Old real estates

...

Al-Mutanabbi

...

Leaves of the bitter times

...

A black cassette

...

Green Lincoln town car

...

Old songs of Abdul Majeed Abdullah

...

MBC radio FM

…

Saud Al-Dosari

…

Evening conversations until late at night

…

The Thursday night

…

Ahmed Alhamed voice everywhere

…

30th Street

…

Fahrenheit perfume

…

White car phone with black buttons

…

Sheraton Hotel

…

Takhassusi Steet

…

The afternoon coffee

…

Kareem coffee

…

Bourj Al Hamam

…

Riyadh…

The city of the silent love.

It is a city which I chose to shed light on a specific time phase in it. It has a beautiful influence on my heart and has unforgeable memories. I lived in it the most beautiful days of my life with the family, friends, and other people I love. They departed from this world to another one way more beautiful.

Monaco

It is a different city.

It consists of a mountain inlaid with diamonds that shines at night. It is the city of luxury and splendid yachts.

Celebrities usually take it as a domicile.

It is a very elegant place, very quiet, and very very noisy.

It is a city that becomes at night a fair woman
called Grace Kelly.

(**Rome**)

Espresso

...

Heavy traffic

...

The smell of car exhausts

...

 People communicating with their hands a lot

...

People fighting a lot with each other and you discover after that that they are actually joking

...

Beautiful people who do not rely on that in their lives

...

Margarita

...

Happy humans

...

Sounds of cars horns

...

Trevi Fountain

...

The Spanish steps

…

Piazza del Popolo

…

Rome Bus tours

…

Silence

…

It is a historic city and its inhabitants are happy.

In its center, there is the loneliest and saddest building in the world – the Colosseum.

(New York)

Manhattan

…

A yellow taxi

…

Buildings… buildings… buildings

…

Air streams through the buildings

…

All people holding coffee in their hands

…

Newspapers…newspapers…newspapers

…

The Plaza Hotel

…

Broadway

…

Betrayal play for Daniel Craig

…

Black coffee from Starbucks shop at the corner of
the Times Square

…

The red path of love

...

The corner of Flatiron Building

...

The Fifth Avenue

...

It is a modern, gentle city. When you visit it for the first time, you feel as if you have visited it earlier.

(London)

I will write about you later. I am not finished with you, yet…

Ending

Dear reader,

I am proud that you have reached this page... the last page of my journey with you. We, you and me, have spent days together. I feel responsibility towards you and happiness, too.

I would like you to know that when I wrote the texts of the book you are holding in your hands right now, I never intended to publish them one day. I only wanted to write for myself, and nobody was supposed to read them!

When I thought of publishing them, I started collecting my writings from different places and times. Some of them are new while others are old. I ordered the chapters of the book according to their topics to make reading the book and enjoying it an easier experience.

Dear reader,

I would like you to know that I do not consider this book as a complete work because it does not contain all texts and writings I have; I published only what I thought worth publishing in the present time. I still keep for myself hundreds of other sheets of paper that will be published in the proper time. I am also writing other texts because I cannot stand if a day passes without writing at least one word.

Dear reader,

At the end, I would like to dedicate for you all the texts of the book. Choose from them what represents you or echoes something in you, keep it for yourself and give it as a gift for whom you love.

Keep me in your mind when you choose any favorite text from the book, because we might meet someday! And I would like to know from you personally why you picked that piece! Keep it, too, because we might meet me someday. Then I would like you to tell me why you picked it. Keep in mind, too, that you are not the only one in this universe who has experienced such similar feelings and did not write about them or share them with others.

With all love and respect.

Fahad
19/7/2017
12:52 am
Hotel Milestone Kensington –
London